BUT A STORM IS BLOWING
FROM PARADISE

BUT A STORM IS BLOWING FROM PARADISE

poems

LILLIAN-YVONNE BERTRAM

RED HEN PRESS | PASADENA, CA

Book layout by John Nwagwu
Book design by Mark E. Cull

Library of Congress Cataloging-in-Publication Data
Bertram, Lillian-Yvonne, 1983–
   But a storm is blowing from paradise : poems / Lillian-Yvonne Bertram.—1st ed.
     p. cm.
   Includes bibliographical references and index.
   ISBN 978-1-59709-168-8 (alk. paper)
   I. Title.
   PS3602.E7685B88 2012
   811'.6—dc23

2011047114

The Los Angeles County Arts Commission, the National Endowment for the Arts, and the
Department of Cultural Affairs City of Los Angeles partially support Red Hen Press.

First Edition
Published by Red Hen Press
www.redhen.org

ACKNOWLEDGMENTS

Many thanks to the following journals where these poems have appeared, some in earlier versions: *Alligator Juniper, Bellingham Review, Cutthroat, Harvard Review, Indiana Review, jubilat, la fovea, Mid-American Review, Narrative Magazine, OH NO,* and *Sou'wester.*

GRATITUDES

(As if my thanks for all the love, support, blessings, and strength that have come my way could fit in this space.)

Mom, dad, and my bother: This is for you. Thank you for your patience, love, good sense, and never letting me down.

My partner, Mike Lynch, for loving me, crazybones and all.

Erin Carman, for being my root and rock for so many years.

The Pittsburgh Cohort: S.E. Smith, A.M. Rooney, Zachary Harris, Adam Atkinson, & Ben Pelhan—y'all know what's up. Makin' it happen and keepin' it real.

CMU: Terrance Hayes & Jim Daniels, I am incredibly indebted to you both for making this path possible and for your endless patience.

The Cave Canem family: Especially Duriel Harris, Ruth E. Kocher, Krista Franklin, and Major Jackson.

UIUC: Tyehimba Jess, thank you for never letting me back down and always hooking me up. My homeboy, Matt Minicucci, who helped me keep on during those years. Brigit Kelly, for your generosity and kindness. With love, always, to Michael David Madonick.

Williams: Immeasurable thanks to the Gaius Charles Bolin Fellowship, the English Department, Africana Studies, and the MCC. Special thanks to the amazing Karen Swann.

Many thanks to Vermont College of Fine Arts Post-graduate Manuscript Workshops, the Bread Loaf Writers' Conference, and the Montana Artists Refuge.

Thank you Kate Gale, Red Hen Press, and Claudia Rankine for thinking highly of my work.

And to the other cook in this kitchen, the realest real deal for whom thankful is too clumsy a word: Steve Davenport.

Contents

{ONE}

The Body Deformed by Tidal Forces

Darkness still here, hunkered against the trees.
Spring so uneasy this year.
No matter morning's boundary culling our bodies,
another romantic passage assaults us!
O limp future centered on this body!
In the model solar system, planets suspend & twirl
as if from a spider's whirl.
The quantum in backpedal, in decline, spring so un-
gripping this year. Bored mouth. Bored fingers.
The umpteenth day/night running like such—
truly, truly—this troubling with physics!
Not still winter, not yet anything.

O thuggish awakening.
All planets but this one were named after gods.

I MEET MY FATHER AT THE END OF AMERICA

Largely as he had painted it:
a bismuth yellow field
of chuckle-colored barns

upturned as if shook down
from a beach bucket above.

In his hand, return passage
to Maastricht. He intends to sail
backward into himself.

How easily I glide to him
& we stand together.
A fair daughter from an even
fairer son. He scarcely

seesaws his wrist over herds
of ghostly beasts. Once this.
Once that. His palm directing
my eye to the melting light

of skeletal New Harmony,
the shining white *waapaahšiiki,*

its bloated banks & the river road
trees bent with webworm

in late summer when leaving
is led by one's own shadow.

—*after Bin Ramke*

Regards, from Middle Country

∞

Let me speak on what I can.
This deerland's a whole new knowing.
Can't wiggle fingers at your waist
call it a skirt. The train barely bothers
a howl through town. Corn confers
in the thinnest of winds a hum divine.
On burn days every bit of breath
a shallower canyon a horse the poorer
for it. Vision occurs in the brain not
the chatty eyes. Live lonesome
for a moon illusion you sit with awhile
and still see wrong.

∞

What rubs between
the skirted legs
of the girl
on the bike
blinds like a gun shot
over the fields
as she lifts it.
What if not space
holds together
fingers. Ask the rock
quarry *can you ignore*
the splitter at your walls?
Could it say
you would not
know it. The tea begs
milk me sugar.

∞

Route YY, mile marker
            XXX, photograph

this predictable sundown,
scolding through
those windows so predictably
        missing their panes.

When you leave here, leave in a flashy car
and wave goodbye—photograph
that clapboard barn

& those grey geese
dripping field marsh down on us
as they fly the hell out of this year.

In a letter to you
        before my mind was off
the birds,
I wrote exact what I saw: *they flew the hell*
out of this year.

In Leaving My Lover Teaches Me Half a Bible Story

Inside my heart's blackening egg, where some might say they see
    a lake of fire,   or,   Asmodeus picking his fingernails
in the doorframe of my wedding nights

I see a slack-jawed barn down on its knees, cradled up against
the interstate. You know the one. Call it clairvoyance

or sorrow from self-undoing.

Mutable water signs or what-
    ever. Lion/lamb of the calendar. My sound denatured
—all cluck and bang—knowing

the too-late clang of this road travels long and longer. My mouth

is full of permissions, more sleepy talk of killing
    this man or that man. I stuff my lips with wine and livers.

Inside I see a flock of wasps
    buoying the carcass of a deer over Nameless Creek,

over Mad River, past Mount Comfort

& up the knoll where they bury it in the dirt of the barn floor—
        flinty & stalwart. Watch its body vanish

in the mouths of shimmery creatures that slip flesh from bone.

In some years this deer will want to rise & see what kind of day it is.

Will it still be March? Will Tobia be walking still? & Sarah
        with her drowsy hips padding the earth on her *nth* husband's grave?

Knocking this way then that way, the bones curl up from crisp dust
        to ring
with the hard laughter. Always a kind of wailing.

Medicine Lake

What I invent is for you to talk to me when all I hear is the petite cat's ghost
I pretend your mass is here redshifting with the rigs pumping their brakes a
little closer than we'd think they'd be Out in the country where we are still
inventing ourselves and the empty room I never got around to so I call it *your
room* I say *you can have it* You're in Hugo's NeverNeverLand strong-arming
Russian Olives from the ridge to the chipper & what's a promise to a crow in
hungry season I practice my fist to mimic physical phenomena The *heart thing*
your father grappled last week They say *fist* is about the size of *heart* but only if
you're a kid By the time his heart hears about Saturn's new ring its blood will
have dilated & receded through space Imagine you are overshadowed by debris
so large you miss the debris entirely A galaxy of sandhill tracks flowering in the
snowy mud along Medicine Lake & your father calling out oldest to youngest
the names of his seven children

IN THE DEMOCRACY OF GOODS,

there is no equal & I am a candidate
    for closure: my hand is down

in my *Full Moon Saloon*,
a coin

            thrust in the potter's wheel

where the jukebox
is the most complex woman
around   where nine in ten

women do not pad the other side
of the bed, or put the eggs
           & milk on credit

—my camera, my magic box
    of accident, duplicates the real

that is not real enough: nine in ten
women know the exact name

of the pill
they are taking

& all women keep track
of their jukebox growth—

I know it goes against so much
                    that I touch myself

bring up fluids demand
that you look

—open the shutter long enough
and light swoops become

naked bodies   in the corn
pits.

BEHIND THE CHRISTIAN DOOR

And when is the state gonna pay us? And
when is the state gonna pay us? And when is
the state gonna pay us? And when is the
state gonna pay us? And when is the state
gonna pay us? And when is the state gonna
pay us? And when is the state gonna pay us?
And when is the state gonna pay us? And
when is the state gonna pay us? And when is
the state gonna pay us? And when is the
state gonna pay us? And when is the state
gonna pay us? And when is the state gonna
pay us? And when is the state gonna pay us?
And when is the state gonna pay us? And
when is the state gonna pay us? And when is
the state gonna pay us? And when is the
state gonna pay us? And when is the state
gonna pay us? And when is the state gonna
pay us? And when is the state gonna pay us?
And when is the state gonna pay us? And
when is the state gonna pay us? And when is
the state gonna pay us? And when is the
state gonna pay us? And when is the state
gonna pay us? And when is the state gonna

pay us? And when is the state gonna   pay us?
And when is the state gonna pay us?   And
when is the state gonna pay us? And   when is
the state gonna pay us? And when is   the
state gonna pay us? And when is the   state
gonna pay?

MOON ILLUSION ECLOGUE

In this burnt haze, the chroma
    of car dealership lights
        lunges out over the road:

a car-full of boys yells
    nigger piglet at the girl walking home
        from the late shift at taco bell, her hair

pulled back in a moon so tight
    her forehead throbs, then the boys
        race a yellow and bump

a man on his bike through a patio
    crowded with diners–
        microwave theory begins

the crumble under its own weight
    & dusts us all with the cancer
        where everything we see goldens

before we die—a perfect picture: someone's mother,
    someone's daughter, a ruddy moon
        tacked above a building necked with vines:

the girl still walks & glances
over-shoulder at a prairie burn

& not far behind her: two cop cars parked
cheek to cheek
in the unlit corner

of a parking lot, where one hand traces
ragged craters onto another,
traces the sound of a rabbit

raking through railroad bramble,
the sipping from their blue sodas
not silent but full with want

& in the poorness of this night—the moon spun
in its low chamber, its troubled house,
burns out over some yonder fire.

APOCRYPHA

The story can be simplified. Lustful Asmodeus
          drives off another lover who takes with him

all his seed. My next sleep's dream: a witch
          comes disguised as Mary Undoer of Knots

teaches me a spell of binding, a spell
          of disorientation. *To mix up a demon, crisp the sullen*

blood of organs. Fire a fish heart and liver on the cinders
          of your lonesome hearth. Mutter a bitter chant all night.

My hands roam, knot a foul & angel-less fog.
          As it should, my stitched sun comes up and still it is

Monday my lover leaves, takes with him all his seed.
          Forget the weak science of fish hearts. I choose a girl

on a bike to follow home. A girl who thinks, surely,
          she is different from all other girls. A girl in the dairy aisle.

A girl everyone knows. Now the girl on the news.
          Anyone's organs will do. We are claimed by middle country

where the river is cooked to steam in the factory belly
        & every quivering shadow is missing its father.

This year we pray for a newer, more improved, magic.
        She wants to turn down her suntinted road. The corn gone

to seed with mutts routing in the rail bed.
        She wants to go home but I will not let her.

I cuss and cuss. Into her ear with my blurry song.

The Night My Dead Dog Comes Back

It wasn't cancer, turns out. Or my fears
of dropping her down the stairs the way it happened
in a dream, her hindquarter snapping
bloodless as a fish stick.

It wasn't anything but the universe skipping
ahead somewhere near the end and coming
back on the middle it took with it—the dust
and stars and dogs, something *extragalactic*

in the mix—and no, the cancer, how it filigreed
her esophageal strands same year that boy
from high school seized up behind the steering wheel
of his benz—was never more than occasional

transient clusters unaccounted for in the galaxy
moving on toward some blacker denser point
—luckily,

my dog tells me, in this new real none of that
was real—I didn't lay my body among tarbushes
outside Acropolis to let some *Marcos* pull down
my top with the hand that wasn't unzipping—

—even the *julienne* I make of my thumb & peppers
tonight streams away from me to some
cosmic core—there was no embracing this or

that trickylittlelie the nine-tenths moon told,
hung like a warhead over a child lunging toward
a piece of cheese in an outstretched hand—the endless
blues, the bridge out and out and out

for good—where *Cornus Canadensis* douses our boots
in infinite nuclei, a just-bloomed connection comes
alive among clumpy distributions of the stellar.

Golfing in the Dark with Old Man Heart

We never get to say goodbye after each ball

For the chewing horse stands far in the field & Old Man

doesn't get sentimental about practice tee-offs

Hear dirts of the prairie fly from us

like so much quantum dust whisking in the eyes of deer

Old Man checks his heart

Where is the pause carried   Who was more tender, him

or his wife   This pause like a child at the edge

of a crisp and folding galaxy   carried too fast into the ever

into the let go   deer-white light

Circles in the Sky

I want to want
to tell you
about dakota
where I

rev
the wolf

in my throat
zone
of avoidance

buffaloing
the sky above

my throat twinned
to twin fish

a dinosaur
of black
in the druggist's back
yard

licking pisces
from the galactic
plain's boot-
black hills

a cello
spruce & shined
spits a dirge

for every
torched library
extinct star

& keystone
keychain that falls
to the floor
of the car

between
the pedal &
the metal

the way cross
country
has always
been

lugnutted
to a wheel carto-
graphic

Queen City Fractal

A whole world stacked in a garage, a
gauge. Birds at the feeder, a gauge.
Someone walking a Buffalo beach on
Christmas, waves way beyond the piled
tremors of ice.

      That person is married now,
done thinking of the minute.
The sum of all birds at the feeder
bird plus two bird plus four bird plus bbbbirdddd
better expressed as $\left(\frac{bird + 1}{2}\right)$ x *bird*
& what did the savvy knight demand but
one penny for the first bird, two for the
second, and four for the third. He
demands a single *gauge boson*: the carrier of
forces, feather alone that flies.

      He uses the feather to decorate
flight alone, requests only a strength
carrier. First bird's one penny, two the
second, four for three, celebrated as
bird over bird over bird to take as his
reward.   That persona is wedded
now, made to think minute. Somebody

that walks a Buffalo beach on
Christmas walks the way of waves beyond
the accumulated vibrations of ice. Enter a
worldly garage. Birds in
the feeder, another meter. That person
marries now.

THE SCIENCE OF HEART

I receive the heart

not-red. Not pulsing and warm. But grayish brown
with yellowed clumps, yellow like ordinary chicken fat

and

the lab technician explains to me

no one keeps around live hearts.

What happens

when the heart, or any other organ,
is removed from the body—it lives a mayfly life.
Blood blooms out of the organ into flight,
and it dies. It takes a few hours but it dies.

Transplant medicine can keep a heart viably alive,
but even if it walks it into another body it has already
had little deaths.

(How to check myself for some-dead heart.)

I take it home anyway.

It's not that the heart and brain compete

but the brain is the major shareholder in a plan that must always

go according to plan.

The science of fainting as I understand it:

An involuntary emergency response

in which blood can't climb to the brain as fast as the brain needs for it

in which the brain diverts the body's blood

from all elsewhere in the body directly back to the brain

in which the brain prioritizes its desperations above all else.

Proposition A: The heart is smelly. It smells of clay.

Corollary: To properly observe the heart outside the body, it must be silenced of blood and preserved.

Proposition B: The heart does not smell of blood, or of the absence of blood. One won't ever smell the heart smelling of blood.

Corollary: Preservatives make it possible to properly observe and examine the heart outside the body, as in a classroom setting. Even then, to prevent the growth of mold, the preserved heart will require constant refrigeration.

Proposition C: In all likelihood, the closest one will ever get to a heart close enough to smell, it will be under the condition that the heart is dead.

Corollary:

In this dream,

The bride shakes on her mermaid dress.

Dream corollary: {Ø}

And in the other,

I drive a beautiful black car far too fast. I park it, lose the keys, and forget where I parked it on a very hot day. All this I try to explain to a brother-in-law, whose baby was buckled in the back seat.

Dream corollary: Carelessness always my darkest dilemma.

Dinner with the heart:

It is every companion here that could be here.

The heart has a prehistoric beak.

Now I see how it could be so many animals.

The more I look the more its color turns

a color I know.

The science of heart as I

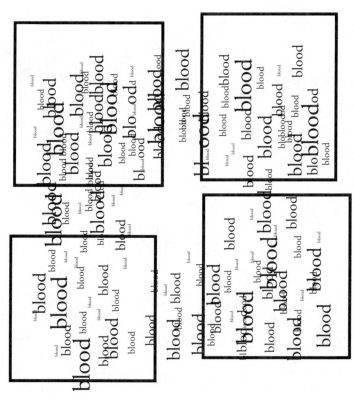

understand it.

There is a smell:

"Too blood." I won't talk about it, but I know where to get it when I want it.

Bisect the heart.

Hold each half in hand as a common coconut.

Bang it together.

Rhythm of your own choosing.

{Two}

Account of the Apparitions

—the end of billion dollar days came. It was like
    old times
again,
      those old times everyone knew had occurred
but no one alive had lived them—

    my old man, he held a lamp by his head &
peered into the darker corners of our house where
dust mixed
      its potions of small & infinite clouds.
We would know to call it the Summer of Sorrow.
    The Fall of Painted Statues with Paint
Worn Off,
        when every girl
& friend
      needed an abortion. Even me.
We all had one. Two. Hundreds.

It was all so hip.   All so cruel. It was
    a hip kind of cruel. It was a club.

    We took blankets sewn
with thinning economic plans and called them

shawls. When we wore them,

we looked like movie stills, stretching to fit
        the screen. We looked like faded slide film,
tattooed symbols behind our ears:

                                    the $

and *Eye of Horus*—

GHOST TOWN

Cottonwoods release their seeds   in droves & mixed mountain breeds of dog go

    run the gravelly Quartz Lode Rd, catch-

                ing seedlings in their mouths. Someone's raccoon-

Labrador bellows.   The sooty grouse Shepard

        haunts the corpse of a smelter.   A logger's

moose-Dalmation mutt stomps its feet.   Two grizzly

        poodles: one black, one white, bark at each other

                                in unison

inbred hips fling their legs out at

obtuse angles like a model plane

built by a child's hand the force of movement

threatens to flip them apart as they give

every car a chase until it approaches

the highway junction turnoff.   My right

eyelid's upper corner twitches in time   with the bank of clouds just moving in

over the three-knuckle ridge. Tonight I am

in one of those cars speeding toward the junc-

tion, and my keychain compass says I am

heading south.   The man driving thinks he

is doing the hijacking but it is I who grip

his wrist like a bear   and through my thousand

darknesses

hear my dark

-self growl *drive, motherfucker, drive.*

THE NEW NEW THING

First I toast a pancake
in the toaster. Then respond
to my brother via email: *Yes,*

I think you are spending too much time
with the potters. I mean, the models.
Them and their silky vaginas.

What with the dream
like snow & macabre icicle
this could be a day of reckon-

ing. I begin in the bathroom,
hammering at the bathtub,
underneath which I find

another startlingly purple bathtub.
All the hammering makes my teeth ring
like a Big Ten weight room. Me entangled

on the other side of the universe
sits up in her chemise, gasps,
hammers away. Me and Me

are getting quantum. Me and Me probe
harder & faster, making promises
to Me and Me as we go and in all
our favorite colors.

We will be strict vegans at the edge
of a humbly beautiful town,
our speech snug elegies. To be brave

in the face of terror and remain quiet
about our wealth. We will learn
more about the cosmos then apply

that knowledge to the arts.
To quote after and at length, maxims
unknown to most, reflecting applause

in our faces & never our hands. To always
hold hands. I'll marry you, Me says,
and you'll marry Me. We want no other.

I Was a Barking Dog

I was a thing once.   A coyote
routing the timber
at the river's edge.

Then, the river's edge.

January's frigid waistcoat
slinging my belly
low over the fields.

The fields?
Barked with ice.

I coyote fell in love
with grackle, a common icterid
in decline. For this I would
take breaking

over meanness.
But I became its meanness
too and in the dark
lost its trail.

I was a poor-eyed
coyote overtired with a state
of haunting that feels
like desire.

When I was a woman
and my lover was a man
I did not hunt in pairs.

I did not have these fields
to choose from.

And yet I wished for them.

My sleep as a woman
was inferior & menstrus.
I was all reason & my reason
was unjust.

Grew bored of thinking
with myself, these pictures
of my living imagination.

Everything there? Inaccurate.

Beyond my ability
to say how.

I wasn't many things.

Coyote not quite
          Cóyotl.

Not quite a wolf
though known as the wolf
of the prairie.

PASTORAL FOR EFFECTIVE TEACHING

We must head
to the hilltop—uncostume.
And I don't mean
in the swanlike way.
Raise a rocks around a sinking.
I mean: the night is so helplessly
white. Girl and Boy
cling together
at the roadbottom—
a dangerous turn.
In the bushes hear one thing
eating another.
Glimmer goes the thinpan
moon. The decorative
hillside
where weeds lie waiting
spring sheep at the end of a season
at the tail end of a mountain
slapped like a whale.
The forest sons
a river's daughter.
You are still wearing
the narrow bridge, Lillian,

slicing up the coyote's paw.
Untake this business
of brilliant chill.

But a Storm is Blowing From Paradise

The form you had not anticipated for life
takes form in life

A stick whittled to water-blue hand swims beneath the snow
for a key   small heart   something that's been dropped

                              You   begin

To think you live in a curved globe—the way everything takes on

a curved shape   curves
          to the space around the shape

Inside the globe: a comely smallish town with real bell-ringers in its bell-towers

streaked with the nippy smoke of days spun   spun   no one can

be lonely with medleys at noon   four   & seven   according to the new   the

new new   new science   we are all made of space curved

curved-shaped-space

        have you noticed how long he's been gone

no one feels the curve of the globe   they are sewing

drinking water   overwhelmed in any number of ways   you   are   in   the

bathroom overwhelmed by the one hair   areolar   that spirals

go after your love tell him you love hurry him through the
cremnitz streets snow wet-hair heavy past coffee shops
bicycles frozen children with sugar cookies pressed against
lamps and each other licking the frosting the moment you
will to be gorgeous and tuning on your tongue like a pearl

And the bell ringer?
His story is as cloudless
as a gun. In the study
of bells he practices
running his arms
up and down the $n!$
permutations of ropes.
He affects his nacreous
whimper for when
the harvesting comes.
Please. I am thirsty.
It's my birthday.

You come kicking   round the corner   in a cloud
of salt   on the snow-taken   side of town

Or you stay behind   stare   at a glass empty on an empty table
promising promise

& what of the weather where he's been gone

Let us say   outside the globe   someone great

& masterful   shaves the globe   surface

with the sharpest

of knives

That in a constant shower he lets it fall is as good a possibility as any

STEEL CITY FRACTAL

Do it again do it do it do it again
jump from the bridge I jumped from
the bridge you still see through me I still steal
see through you, like ardent
light company.
Hear the one about the soles of our feet
they called it "night rescue."
I named this bridge after
you, I named it "Killmekillyou" it's native
American.
I named this street
after you too I named it
"Glassdirtgardenwherepotatoeswon'tgrow."
     The street has your name
Glassdirtgardenwherepotatoeswon'tgrow,
I have named this street it too has your
name and later I named this bridge, you,
I was named to name it "Killmekillyou"
this native born American.
They had to call it the rescuing of night
by our feet and shoe soles
likely some
warm-hearted company like light hopped

from a bridge, you see that to the end.
You still see me who again still stole
through you to work it again, again,
the bridge it jumped from me.

GICLÉE SELF-PORTRAIT WITH MOUNT RUSHMORE

Sigh. It is a
perfect rendition.
Every key so
sharp, so exquisite-
ly depressed. For
Dad, I snap a
washed-out flick:
*me & Teddy wish you
were here!* Ground a
penny to badlands
pancake.

      Because I am
brown & traveling
alone and it is still
the age of deer
ticks, *let me show you
something*, & other
nuttiness—I must
remain suspicious
of everything. Will

Wall be waiting at
the exit *(what city
did she say she
tracked through which
canyon what did her
license indicate)*?
     Today I am so
proud to be of a
recognizable
nation. Here is my
presidential
revelation, stoning
through one of his
or his or his
avatar ears:
     *Every now and
then, I sing "Ol Man
River" very quietly
to myself.*

Am Looking For

desperately,
children: a
toaster, many
coupons & 14
egg cartons are
offered; I need
men's ties, a
queen
frame/headboar
d, chimney
cleaning
supplies, cat
carrier for found
kitten, double
stroller and baby
gates; will trade
for sofa, extra
long: a few
cassettes,
various VHS
films, shingle
remover; am
looking for fake

Christmas tree,
other needed
stuff; needed in
N____ A____:
flea bombs, a
basic beginner's
telescope, copy
of a brief history
of time, daybed,
washing
machine; shirt
and tie or whole
suit would be
perfect! contact
me for an ant
farm & various
items: de-
humidifier &
soccer gloves,
women's black
heels, clipboard,
dog feeding
thingy—three

drinking
pitchers.
Chinchilla dust
& whack-a-mole
to good home.
Bugkiller and
pool vacuum. I
need a couch
and wood stain,
am in desperate
need for
desperate need;
am in desperate
need for 2
controllers for
Nintendo 64,
one unicorn
costume.

Why I Want to Be a Tow Truck Driver

This body makes no
uncommanded sounds.
My reach? Unimaginably
torpulent. See the snowclouds
thrusting over the range
like a cough,
a hardpacked fist? This is how
I come. Free of disguise.
Because life is hard but also
crisp and literary I come
as an exotic vapor comes
in a grove of nuts—
when the devil in his hide
of night has drawn himself up
yards and yards, reaching
like a chokechain. I tell you—
I know my excellence.
I am excellent at my job
and I am excellent at you.
What choice do you have
but to believe anything
I say? I gave a ride
to a girl with her thumb

out like a lollipop
caught in the summer
rain and all I did to her
was give her my card.
I know every kind
of sorry, can plot all form
of survivorship curve.
On time I come when your
heart proves itself
to be a licky-loo bomb
in the razor dark
when I matter the most.
I see the sun and road
for what they are—outbursts
of slutty and grey.

—after ZPH

{THREE}

Hinterland Ham Radio Signals

jettajettajettajettajettajettajettajetta
jettajettajettajettajettajettajettajetta

this is sheridan   over   montepelier?   over

anyone out there

i'm crossing   BNSF   thermopolis, solo *jettajettajetta*

Bighorn   *jettajetta* dark fucking dark

deerlike ghosts

onward to points

tell me what note

lands behind   is this

                    meant to be a travelogue

can someone help teach me

guitar?
                                            expected
            snow at highest elevations

report mountain weirdness, over

        jettajettajettajettajettajettajettajettajetta
jettajettajettajettajettajettajettajettajetta
——sorry, you broke up there

                    what is your children like?

jettajettajettajettajettajettajettajetta
jettajettajettajettajettajettajettajetta
jettajettajettajettajettajettajettajetta
jettajettajettajettajettajettajettajetta
wharfing constellations in the noosed wander
jettajettajettajettajettajettajettajetta
jettajettajettajettajettajettajettajetta
jettajettajettajettajettajettajettajetta
jettajettajettajettajettajettajettajetta
limbs so gently sad singing thunderheads
jettajettajettajettajettajettajettajetta
jettajettajettajettajettajettajettajetta
jettajettajettajettajettajettajettajetta
jettajettajettajettajettajettajettajetta
wrecked my atv up telephone ridge
jettajettajettajettajettajettajettajetta

jettajettajettajettajettajettajettajetta
jettajettajettajettajettajettajettajetta
jettajettajettajettajettajettajettajetta
anyone monitor this frequency
jettajettajettajettajettajettajettajetta
jettajettajettajettajettajettajettajetta
jettajettajettajettajettajettajettajetta
jettajettajettajettajettajettajettajetta

free phrase

Trying to stay wake here!
 universe splitting tonight over!

Crisis my love crisis I came for this didn't I *jettajettajettajetta*
Road now open   over   clearance height*jettajettajettajetta*required
                                 over
I believe the car as *jettajetta* the body is what makes America great

Did you say savage   over *jettajetta*   or civil   over

81

"I AM TRYING AS HARD AS A HUMAN"

I am the girl at the 4-H
sow steering practical event
in the bow tie
western white shirt
tucked under black jeans
buckled high
and my pig won't stop
urinating in the ring
won't be turned
in its staunch little circle
for the judge
who wants to see
me smile. My friend, do you
not ever wish instead
to be a cat
the killing kind of cat
making off
with other children's
swiftless pets clenched deftly
in our jaws?
How I have withered
in my life as a sow steerer
& in my life as a marmot

sunning on a rock beneath
Sacajawea Peak
& even as braided little
Sacajawea herself
secreting from her mother
the neighbor man
who snaps her
bathing suit straps
who in summer
among the strawberries
gets his bearings behind her
can't stop himself
from pluck & sting
says what a big booty
she'll have a big booty
by the time she's a nurse
or volleyball player
or whatever. Whatever.
That booty. That indemnible
booty she'll think it's too big
but it won't be.
And my other friend
don't you ever wish

instead that we were
the two hands clapping
a pair of shi tzu's
to the chow bowl?
Or the telephone switcher
beneath the satellites
of switches butting in
on the "hot" lines,
butting in on the carousel
of LA → NY lovers
living on Tokyo time
fingering air and licking
syllable after electrified
syllable from the receiver?

After Matthew Zapruder & Michael Martone

IN THE DEMOCRACY OF AFFLICTIONS,

it is fact & well known
  that the white man comes

like a gangster always arrives like a pilgrim
  in turkey's clothing

that when he comes he comes mad
  with the knowledge he comes into

that where man cannot live
  what bird could fare

& the black man knows the way in
  is the way out

that the menu is not the meal
  that the trouble is light

hear him call to you from across
  the supermarket parking lot

suggest that you smile more *shorty*
  if you tried, you could brighten

and what greater purpose is there
        for a woman to have—

the face an announcement
        —a bulb burning contrary to

night branches after a fire has fallen
        and ash dampens with nightdew—

careful not to look past
        the next footfall in the valley

forced up by the wind
        the pale side of the leaf

to face you: not the wound on the tree
        its barked over   evidence of illness

but the gully
        where you must go to gather wood

something troubled is breathing.

Phenomena Not Foreseen

there is no way to be modest

his fingers climbed in   by that summer's swollen lake
                the canoes

kneaded against the dam   like children desperate to see
over each other   at the drag race

I bent him to cello and back again   climbed out
of the lakebed
                sought
the longest pause between the known
elements &

dark matters of design: those particulates causing all the trouble maybe we laughed ourselves into halos   I adjusted my shorts

talked vaguely about vague things

or I was already ten years from then   riding

shotgun in a convertible

my hair out and head   exhausted on big ideas that broke

like a hoof on the back of a fly   night game no more

than stretched light

blur of little leaguers

batting epically at the cosmic

abundance

Satori

What the body does not know
    it just invents: a girl bucking herself to sleep
        on the back of her hand.

Or the sound of a chair creaking
    is the sound of a man
        having a heart attack

in the lobby.
    On some airplane
        an ink pen leaks on pants

pressed in a suitcase. A woman
    shifts her leaky blood
        into the twice circulated air.

In the poorest county
    behind a house on palettes
        our piebald dog

wails at the line of junipers
    rushing at him, and the valley
        pulls its long arm down

on the prickle of starlight.
    The man and his architecture grasp
        for semblance of rhythm:

a balcony's pendular love,
    the triple-eight knots
        of a torn bedsheet.

Someone should call his wife
    made a pale deer
        by downshifting

night. Made a pale window
    facing the pond made rain
        choking on glass.

Rex Mundi, or,
Watching My Father Paint What He Knows
of the Horizon

On his cotton duck barn bottoms signal to the vein-blue sky
falling back up. Others riveted on their barn skulls

cough a geometric alphabet. How could he forget
this orange-deep slip of land, *grootmoeder* pinning

sheets, her knees in the crisp plié of Ohio's horseshoe bend
knuckling its abysmal barges.

Soon, my father says, *the Green River shale will be choked for oil.*
He would know:

upstate, our basement pantry equipped with beans & water
bought on sale.

Still in their plastic—undershirts from the remainder rack.
Pyramids of batteries.

I chew a fingernail until it stings like a swallow of frigid air.

Remember that we are dust. To my pocket of dollars
he fastens a row of Old Holland teeth, cremnitz & leaden.

What the Elk Told Me

Following the creek through the canyon searching for the mine
the mine led me to the elk. I saw the elk who was not bothered by
how I continued after it. We walked up and up the ridge. I learned
the elk is not a bear. The elk is not a wolf nor a cat. The elk is not
a declaration a girl with hips pressed to the spring-covered ground
though I thought it might be or it could be something that perhaps
not an elk at all should be. That is a song. Hips are a song. The elk
is not a hip though it has two.

          The elk is not a trap with its hips. I
am a trap with my hips. The camera is a trap with its hips too. When
the elk saw I was not going to leave it spoke and told me that I am
not a camera though most days I act as one. The camera is a costume
and a costume is not an elk. The elk can never be a costume. What
need does an elk have to pretend. Yet the elk knows I must pretend.
Alpaca keeping said the elk is a costume. Keeping a handful of al-
pacas is never the real thing.

          This is the
wisdom of the elk. The wise elk looked at me with its even darker
eyes. I have been told that I too have elk-like eyes especially in win-
ter and I could see that its eyes were darker than mine darker even
than my brother's eyes who is not my twin but sometimes I sense
him like such. When I asked the elk about birthing she said I was
a sorry thing to have to ask. I said to the elk *I am wanting to know*

the size of my heart. Can you tell me is my heart the size of you? This was possible said the elk if I could carry large things on my back then surely I could carry a large or heavy heart on my back. But the elk could not say if my back was good for carrying. Then the elk asked me what it was I carried in front of my eyes. I told the elk I carried these things to see better that I cannot see well
on my own

without them. Not like the elk. For miles the elk sees through and past the timberline when the sun and clouds move just right sees the game trail it must take through wolf territory to the spring made from melting snows where its offspring sleeps. The elk could see that it was starting to snow and that I had never before seen or knew to know snowfall in june though the elk did not know it was june. The elk could see that I was lost. The elk told me *up is mountain down is home* and that is how she left me there.

Jack Mountain Fractal

On the mean side of the canyon
in the tunnel mouth
the coyote skull grins with sap
picking jukebox from its claws
hung up on the door to flesh.
H_0: *Hubble constant.* Speed
at which the universe is moving
my hand closer to what
I should not touch. Is it wicked
to want trophies.
I saw me see the eyeless
animal
in the June snow
see me resemble the wrong thing
                                    see me resemble
the wrong animal
in the June of snow
I saw me of the seeing of the eyeless
wicked to wanting of trophies.
Of what I should not touch
the universe is moving my hand closer.
H_0: *I constantly resemble the incorrect.*
I saw that I saw an eyeless animal.

In the snow in June the universe
speeds nearer to the claws of those
hung upward on the door to the
flesh, its weapon of picking.

PARTING THE SMOKE CURTAIN ONTO A CURTAIN OF SMOKE

Radiowoman declares *Our strategy is to remain*. So say it as if you are Butte's lady of the mountain with a million years of sump to say to say it sounds true. If only I had such power, rabia so simple as to divinate the concentric tumors of undulate cosmos. A woman dies the same death on the same day at the same age as her mother died her death. When is the breast not elliptical mystery or the grief that walks different on everyone but just the flesh itself. The divided continental where I part the Bitterroot clouds. A shiny little number fists around the guardrail of Beartooth astrology, gives it a godlike squeeze. I saw it from afar. I saw it fall where everything falls. Under the Dipper. In the aspen grove on a bed of shed horns.

$\{H_0\}$

Ring of fire   then the planet cooled   sleeping
      through it   all   the planet's people

There are things that happen nightly

Agonies   of dusty collisions—that's what there is
to look back upon

Forward America, forward with as many grapes
in your mouth as you can
        with your
    rollerskates   cornfields
redshifting into the future
       & hair modestly clinging to lips in the morning

outside the subway   because he loves so absolutely   *Blaze*
the color of my hair   he'll call me   *King*
& let me call him
on one condition

I purchase my token. Descend.

If I choose not to hear him, does he just not
speak?

If I tell him to go, does he go?   How would you
know?

Wait—before you check the lab results, tell me—is the rat dead,
alive, or 50% of both?

I purchase my token. Descend

something inside me grows frowny, inflamed. Entropy
or another word at play.

I run around animal curious
        hold my hair to closing car doors, my fingertip
to the stapler underside   push up in little pulses.

For all the *Sturm und Drang*, there is a name for our puzzle.

Once mixed, molecules speed up. Inhabit the body in outrageous
concoctions. Little blasts of solar light.

Event horizon or brackish tornado froth?

There is similar evidence for both

tremendous boom   & everyone is feasting.

It's how we got here.

Stars gobbling stars.

NOTES

"I Meet My Father at the End of America" incorporates a line from a poem by Bin Ramke.

"Regards, from Middle Country" borrows from Marjorie Perloff's book *Wittgenstein's Ladder*. Somewhere in *The Black Aesthetic*, leaving in a flashy car is mentioned.

"In Leaving My Lover Teaches Me Half a Bible Story" incorporates a line from Terrance Hayes. In "Boy in a Video Arcade" by Larry Levis, "some see a lake of fire at the end of it." It also was inspired by the work of Brigit Kelly.

"Golfing in the Dark with Old Man Heart" is for Michael David Madonick.

According to Wikipedia, "gauge bosons are bosonic particles that act as carriers of the fundamental forces of nature."

Cóyotl, in "I Was a Barking Dog," is Nahuatl for coyote.

"Pastoral for Effective Teaching" glosses some lines from the song "The Crane Wife" by The Decemberists.

The title "But a Storm is Blowing From Paradise" is a line by Walter Benjamin, regarding the Klee painting *Angelus Novus*.

"Why I Want to Be a Tow Truck Driver" was inspired by the poem "Why I Want to Be an Accordion Player" by Zachary Harris, and glosses a line from a song by Josh Ritter.

The title "I am trying as hard as a human" is a line in a poem by Matthew Zapruder. A conversation with Michael Martone contributed to the writing of this poem.

"What the Elk Told Me" incorporates a line from the song *Blue Flame* by Josh Ritter. The phrase "up is mountain, down is home" was told to me by a builder in Basin, Montana, near Jack Mountain.

"Parting the Curtain of Smoke onto a Curtain of Smoke" is the title of an essay section in the chapter "Burning Montana: Richard Ford's *Wildfire* and Regional Crisis" by Tamas Dobozy in the collection *All Our Stories Are Here: Critical Perspectives on Montana Literature*.

H_0 refers to the Hubble constant, a value which is derived from Hubble's Law describing "the velocity at which various galaxies are receding from the Earth is proportional to their distance from us" (Wikipedia).

These poems were informed by Timothy Ferris's book *The Whole Shebang*.

BIOGRAPHICAL NOTE

Lillian-Yvonne Bertram has been a Bread Loaf Writers' Conference work-study scholar and a writer-in-residence at the Montana Artists Refuge, and she is a Cave Canem alumna. Her poetry has appeared in *Black Warrior Review, Callaloo, Gulf Coast, Harvard Review, Indiana Review, Narrative Magazine, Subtropics,* and other journals. She received first place in the 2011 Summer Literary Seminars poetry contest, won *Gulf Coast's* Donald Barthelme Prize for Short Prose, and received second place in *Narrative Magazine's* poetry contest. Bertram is a graduate of the writing programs at Carnegie Mellon University and the University of Illinois at Urbana-Champaign. She was a 2009-2011 Gaius Charles Bolin Fellow at Williams College, where she taught creative writing and literature. She currently lives in Salt Lake City, Utah.